INTO THE LOOKING GLASS
BY
GLENDA C. FINKELSTEIN

A collection of short stories and poetry

Plant City Florida

Published by Final Destiny Press
A Division of Final Destiny Productions
Plant City Florida 33565

Cover Design: Tony E. Finkelstein

Cover Art: Nicola Cuti

Edited By: Tammy Ferrante

ISBN: 978-1-61364-074-6

PRINTED IN THE UNITED STATES OF AMERICA

A Note to the Reader,

This collection of short stories and poetry covers various aspects of my inspiration and creativity in writing and is broken up into three sections: Flights of Fancy, Life, and Faith. Each section has its own unique purpose in my life. **Flights of Fancy** is the imaginative side from simple 'what if?' to 'fantasy adventures' and the awe and wonder of discovery. **Life** encompasses the triumph and tragedy of living and loving. **Faith** is a reflection upon not only our relationship with God, but with the human spirit's ability to overcome and encourage.

Each story will have a brief explanation as to what prompted me to write it, and some have a history all their own. Several that are included in this compilation have been previously published not only in other collections and are indicated at the end of the story or poem with the appropriate first printing information credits, but have become films.

It is my hope that these pages will not only entertain you, but also touch you, and inspire you to pursue your own dreams.

Sincerely,

Glenda C. Finkelstein

TABLE OF CONTENTS

FLIGHTS OF FANCY

LIFE

FAITH

FLIGHTS OF FANCY

Perfect Copy started out as a short story written after a dear friend asked me to contribute to an upcoming anthology called, "Writers for Relief" the proceeds benefiting the Red Cross. I was inspired by the controversial headlines of the day regarding cloning and stem cell research.

Before I could submit the story an opportunity to turn it into a short film literally fell into our laps. I pulled the story and replaced my contribution with a poem, "The Futility of Hate" which is also included in this compilation. I turned the story into a 15-minute script that by the end of filming became a 33-minute short film. The original short story has been lost, but included in this collection is the first chapter of the novelization based upon the feature length script.

Our filmmaking journey began when my husband and I and three other gentlemen joined forces to become Final Destiny Productions. With the help of friends and co-workers that we bribed with coffee and donuts, two SAG actors, and our community including the Pentagon, "Perfect Copy," the film, became a reality. I played the lead character and her clone. I did my own stunts, went under make-up and never worked so hard and had so much fun in my life. We started principal photography in November 2006 and released the finished film in October of 2007. We were accepted at the Melbourne Independent Film Makers Festival in November 2007 where we were nominated for Best Dramatic Short. It was at the festival that we received a phone call from a Producers Rep in California who wanted to take the short film to feature length with a twelve million dollar budget. At the writing of this introduction we are very close to selling the full-length script to another production company. The 33-minute short film is still available on DVD. I hope you enjoy this look into the novelization which includes a portion of the opening sequence that we didn't have the luxury of incorporating into the short film.

PERFECT COPY

Twenty years ago inside a large complex hidden from the prying eyes of the public out in the New Mexico desert, a pharmaceutical company was playing God. There was one person, however, that would not go along with this travesty without doing something. Although she had no idea if her actions would make a difference overall, at least she could change the destiny of one life. Her pleas to the authorities went unheeded as if she were a lunatic crying wolf, which left her in the precarious position of making a personal choice. Usually when people find themselves in overwhelming circumstances they decide to do nothing, but every now and again someone, however unlikely, will choose to act and that action will inevitably lead to change.

Angela Gibbs, housekeeping attendant for World Med Labs, was coming into the baby nursery where twenty plus infants were being kept. Her job was to collect soiled laundry to be cleaned. She looked about the room thoroughly. The only people in the nursery besides the babies were herself and a nurse who was finishing her rounds.

"Hello, Angela," the nurse greeted, unaware of Angela's resolve to steal an infant

"Oh, hi," Angela responded, startled. She had been rehearsing her plan over and over again in her mind. There was a lot at stake. Her and her new husband's life might easily be forfeit, not to mention her beloved father-in-law, Ned.

"I didn't mean to startle you," the nurse apologized.

"It's okay. My mind was elsewhere."

"You just got back from your honeymoon didn't you?"

"Yeah," Angela said, smiling. She was very much in love with her new husband, Alan. They, like so many young couples, had lots of plans for the future.

"Congratulations!"

"Thanks," Angela said, still smiling. Her face could never hide the joy she felt when she thought about Alan.

"Well, got to go. I've got early lunch today. I'm trading shifts with Helen."

"Later," Angela responded waving good-bye. Her smile faded quickly as the nurse walked down the hall.

Angela continued to work with the linens putting the clean ones up in the cabinet, and dumping the dirty linen canisters into her large laundry cart. She watched to make certain that the nurse was out of sight. She looked around one more time at each of the surveillance cameras, took a deep breath, and took up position with her back toward the camera in the corner to block its view of the infants. Her hands were trembling, but it was now or never and she was committed to action.

Inside the Security Control Room there were several bulky black and white TV monitors displaying different views of the facility. The security personnel only glanced at the monitors in between a hand of cards. After all, they were in the middle of nowhere. The closest neighbors were rattlesnakes, roadrunners, and cactus. There was a bulky PC in the corner with a large dot matrix printer on a table nearby. The room, populated by men with cigarettes hanging from their mouths or simply burning in a nearby ashtray, was thick with smoke. The loud noise of the printer could be heard clanking out one report after another along with the tinkling timber of ringing telephones.

Yet, none of the men noticed anything-dubious happening in the nursery. Everything was quiet as it always was, with the exception of the time when a coyote got into the loading docks. The domestic housecleaning staff of which only half could speak English was no trouble because they didn't want to be shipped back to Mexico. The rest of the staff was the nerdy scientist type, and they don't like getting their hands dirty. This promoted an unrealistic atmosphere of security for the work they were secretly conducting at this facility, and would be Angela's single greatest ally for success.

Angela carefully reached into one of the cribs, and took from it an infant who was fast sleep oblivious to the horrors that awaited it should it remain here. She tucked the infant carefully on top of the dirty linens separated by a clean sheet laying another sheet loosely on top concealing the infant underneath. She began to whistle as she commonly did while working in hopes that no one would notice the theft until she was long gone. She was careful to push her cart so as not to wake the infant. She headed out the door of the nursery heading down the hall toward the back service entrance where dirty linens were taken. Waiting near the loading dock was Alan Portman, Angela's husband, in his company tow truck. When she arrived at the loading docks, Angela quickly grabbed the baby and got into the truck. Alan drove off at normal speed hoping to get off the premises before the infant was discovered missing.

The nurse that had finished her rounds when Angela entered the nursery returned to the nursery for a forgotten chart. She noticed that one of the cribs was empty. Slightly unnerved she walked over to the crib to be certain that her eyes weren't playing tricks on her. She wasn't aware of any testing today. She went over to the chart where babies were signed in and out for various reasons, and was curious as to why it was not signed out on the chart. It was standard procedure regardless of the reason the infant was removed or for how long the infant would be gone. She pushed a button to talk on the intercom.

"Security," she called with all the determination of getting things straightened out.

"Security here, how can we help you Naomi?"

"Did another department check out an infant and forgot to sign it out?"

"Let me see," the security guard said, looking over a testing schedule. "No. There's nothing on the duty roster for the nursery infants today."

"Then I need to report one missing."

"Who was the last one in the nursery?"

"The last one in here was Angela Gibbs, the cleaning lady," Naomi answered. The security guard was understandably alarmed, and had visions of being fired running through his mind as he called out orders over the system-wide intercom.

"We have a level-one security breach. Apprehend Angela Gibbs, she's suspected of stealing an infant from the nursery. Repeat. We have a level-one security breach. Lock down the facility!"

The facility alarm system began sounding like a fire alarm going off. Lights flashed all around like a lighthouse beam turning the walls an eerie red. The front gates were closed immediately. Alan saw that the gates were closing and the personnel motioning him to stop. He realized that their secret was out and now he was going to have to crash through the gates if they stood any chance at all in making it out alive.

"Get down on the floorboard. We're going to have to crash the gates," Alan informed Angela. Her face grew pale with fear and her stomach began to twist up in knots.

"What if they shoot, they might hit the baby?"

"Get down! We knew this was a possibility."

"But I had hoped."

"I'll get you and the baby to safety. Just do as I say." Alan's face was full of unwavering commitment to see this through no matter what the cost.

Angela got down onto the floorboard with the baby cuddled close in her arms her eyes never moving from their fixed gaze upon her husband. Alan took a deep breath and began to shift the gears to allow for optimum power and speed. The guards continued motioning him to stop, but Alan ignored them. The security guards fired some warning shots and waited until the last possible moment before jumping out of the way of the speeding truck. Angela squealed in response to the shots as they crashed through the gates. Wood from the gate splintered into fragments that soared through the air. The debris actually assisted their escape due to the fact that it's hard to fire off a shot when your dodging debris.

"Hang in there, baby, I'm getting us out of here!" Alan's tone was reassuring. Angela just gazed up at him with her big blue eyes trusting in the man she married with all her heart. Alan was always a man of his word. His face was set on a course and there was no turning back now.

After they crashed through the gates the guards fired off a couple more shots at the truck, but missed the tires they were aiming at. They radioed back to security headquarters to inform them that their suspects had indeed escaped.

"HQ, this is Gate 4. The suspects just crashed the gate, and are headed for the highway in a tow truck."

"Copy that Gate 4, we're dispatching vehicles to pursue."

Two cars filled with mercenary special agents, who's only goal was to insure World Med Labs remained secure and untouchable by anything or anyone, were dispatched to clean up the leak. The tow truck, however, had a good enough head start that he was able to drop Angela and the infant off at Ned's, his father's trailer, without being seen. She got out of the truck and rushed inside.

"I love you! Never forget that," Alan called after Angela as she ran inside. She glanced back quickly knowing in her heart of hearts that it would probably be the last time she'd see him. Ned ushered Angela quickly into the house and shut the door.

"I'm so sorry," she pleaded with her father-in-law. Her tears began to pour from her eyes, and the infant responded to her emotional state and began to cry.

"Shhh, hush now my child."

"I thought that we could get out together," Angela admitted in defeat.

"Alan and I knew the risks. Now we have to make good in spite of our losses. The only thing that matters now is this child. The car is packed. You know where you're going," Ned coached, as if he were two minutes and one play away from victory.

"But I'll be alone," Angela admitted.

"No, you're not alone," Ned encouraged sneaking a peak at the baby.

"You have to go now," Ned stated sternly. Angela nodded her head in the affirmative. Tears were still evident upon her face. He walked her to the car. She strapped the infant in, and then turned around and threw her arms around Ned.

"I love you," she said.

"I love you, too, darling." Ned smiled a sweet and tender smile. Angela then got into the driver's side of the car and drove away.

Alan continued to lead those following them away. Alan took them on a merry chase down a nearly deserted highway in the exact opposite direction he knew that Angela would be traveling. The cars tried pushing his tow truck off the road, but Alan retaliated with like maneuvers. The whole episode resembled bumper cars. The agents tried cutting him off again, but had to dart back in behind Alan's truck to avoid an oncoming Semi. After the Semi passed they tried one more time to push Alan off the road, but was unsuccessful. They finally grew tired of this game and decided to shoot out his tires forcing him to stop. The moment the truck stopped several agents jumped out and surrounded the tow truck.

"Freeze!" yelled Agent Sawyer, with gun drawn. "Hands on the steering wheel!"

"Why are you shooting at me?" Alan asked with innocent pretense.

"You have stolen merchandise on board," Agent Sawyer replied, annoyed that he even entertained this man's question.

"What merchandise? It's just me," Alan questioned, shrugging his shoulders and smiling.

While Sawyer was questioning Alan, Agent Reynolds checked out the passenger side and storage compartments of the tow truck. There was nothing in any of them.

"He's clean, Sir," Agent Reynolds informed.

"Told ya," Alan quipped, his grin growing ever larger with defiance. Sawyer cocked his weapon. Alan looked a little concerned. "Whoa there, fella. I'm clean."

"Where's Angela?" Sawyer asked. His voice was cold and demanding.

"Who?" Alan asked feigning ignorance.

"Your wife," Sawyer confronted. It was common knowledge that Angela had gotten married, and although Alan knew that they knew, he just couldn't cave. He could see the detached emotionless soldier of fortune inside Sawyer's eyes. It wouldn't matter what Alan said to him, Sawyer was going to kill him. Sawyer wanted to kill him. He was over due for a kill, and Alan was it. At least by being defiant, it'd give Angela a few more minutes to get that much farther away.

"Sorry, you got the wrong guy," Alan said, his tone still trying to be convincing. Although he knew Sawyer saw through his pretense, and his cards started to fold.

"I don't think so. As a matter of fact, I got the right one."

"I'm telling you the truth, man, I don't know any Angela. What'd she do, steel your stash?" Alan questioned, slightly indignant trying to throw him off balance.

"Wrong answer," Sawyer replied, as he fired his weapon killing Alan. Reynolds stood amazed. This was not standard procedure. All suspects were to be questioned at HQ prior to termination.

"Why'd you kill him?"

"Do you really think he'd have told us where his wife went?" Sawyer responded with yet another question, holding up Alan's left hand that held his wedding band.

"Nathan is going to be pissed," Reynolds commented.

"Face it. She's long gone. This was far more than just a snatch and grab, and I've got lots of explaining to do."

"What possessed you?"

"He got under my skin."

"You'll be lucky if Nathan lets you get out of this with your skin."

"I know. I lost control, it won't happen again. Besides it's the first time I've messed up."

"I hate to be negative, but Hitler is more forgiving than Nathan Anderson."

Sawyer just shrugged his shoulders while Reynolds called for the clean-up crew to dispose of the body and the vehicle.

During the theft, Nathan Anderson, Chief Operations Officer of World Med Labs was entertaining an Army Captain to sell him on the use of human clones for black ops purposes. The army had long been looking for the perfect soldier that could be sent into a situation without thought of family or personal safety. Although the enemy had long used suicide bombers that often recruited and brainwashed children as harbingers of death. The Americans and other allied nations still sought a more honorable means of sending troops into certain death situations. World Med Lab clones would offer an opportunity that had never been presented before.

Nathan was sitting at his desk waiting impatiently for a report from Sawyer. This incident could jeopardize his negotiations. Nathan's desk had an old personal computer that looked like a Behemoth compared to today's sleek models, as well as a radio set for communicating with Agents out in the field. Neither had been helpful in ascertaining the status of the stolen infant. His security crew was privy to the radio chatter, but no one had called in to report to him the status of the infant or the perpetrators. He tried to feign calm, but Nathan's chain-smoking gave him away.

Captain Watts sat quietly enjoying a cigar attempting to get a clear read on Nathan's facial expressions. He could tell that Nathan's butt was biting the chair, and having dealt with Nathan on numerous occasions, got a sadistic thrill from the observation. Although Nathan had already tried to raise his agents several times on the radio, they weren't answering. The trepidation of losing the military account was becoming unbearable and was probably the reason why Nathan nearly jumped down Sawyers' throat when he entered his office.

"How'd the capture go?" Nathan questioned, his demeanor was full of fear and anger although no one could have discerned which was truly dictating his actions.

"It didn't sir," Sawyer answered with his head hung low trying to avoid Nathan's piercing dark brown eyes.

"I beg your pardon?" Nathan asked, not wanting to believe what he just heard.

"The suspects got away. Although we killed Alan Portman, her accomplice," Sawyer offered hoping that might soothe Nathan's ruffled feathers.

"Let me see if I get this straight. You lost the cleaning lady, the baby, and killed our only lead to their whereabouts?" Nathan questioned just to make certain he had a clear understanding of what happened. Nathan's eyes zipped back and forth between Captain Watts, who started to look concerned about the situation, and at Sawyer, who knew his life was over. This angered Nathan even more. He could feel the military contract slipping away with each passing moment.

"Yes sir. That's an accurate description."

Sawyer started to bite his bottom lip knowing full well that he had failed. The only question left to answer was would he do it himself or have security haul him off and do it where no one could hear him scream. Nathan began to shake his head back and forth in disgust. Never had Sawyer acted so incompetently. The possibilities of what could happen should the public find out that they have been secretly cultivating clones from stolen DNA for a variety of military and medical purposes nearly shut down his mental processes.

"Do you have any idea what could happen if news gets out about what we're doing here?"

"I know a lot is at stake sir. It won't happen again. I'll make every effort to capture this woman. My team will work night and day until we bring Angela in. I won't fail you again," Sawyer said almost pleading his case.

"How long have you worked for me?" Nathan asked, slightly calmer in tone and demeanor.

"Two years."

"In all that time, how many times have you failed me?" Nathan asked, his temper starting to calm.

"Just this once. I promise, Mr. Anderson, it'll never happen again."

Nathan looked down at the floor, opened his desk drawer, pulled out a gun, and pointed it at Agent Sawyer. A smile of tenderness moved across his face in a terrifyingly cold-hearted maneuver.

"That's right. It won't happen again," Nathan said firing the gun, killing Sawyer instantly. Captain Watts moved slightly to his right to avoid any blood splatter. He just had his uniform pressed. Nathan put the gun away and pulled out a handkerchief to wipe his hands. After methodically wiping his hands, he threw it away in the trashcan. He then followed that with a wet-nap from a BBQ place wiping his hands clean. This cleaning was quite ritualistic in nature and was done with great reverence.

"Although I appreciate your dedication to a no mistake environment, that doesn't fix the problem," Captain Watt's pointed out.

"I assure you Captain this is an isolated incident that'll never happen again. I'll put my best people on search and destroy immediately."

"Very well, my order of twenty specimens still stands. You're certain they won't be ready for two decades."

"Twenty years is the minimum for an order such as yours under current technologies. Although as we continue to make progress in our research, I'm sure we'll be able to greatly reduce that time."

"I want your guarantee that they'll be successful in retrieving your specimen. I can't have an inquiry into my department. There are too many critical operations that could be hampered."

"You have my word."

"Very well, I want a full report on your improved security measures by tomorrow, and an update as soon as you have re-acquired the infant."

"I assure you there's nothing to worry about. I'll handle it personally."

"Understand, Mr. Anderson, I won't tolerate failure."

"I'd stake my life on our success."

"And your life is what the penalty will be should you fail me. I'll be in touch."

Captain Watts got up from the chair and left the facility. Nathan swallowed hard as he watched the Captain leave. He would get the child back, or lie to keep the military contract. Nathan knew he had to beef up security. No one was beyond reproach. He had to come up with personnel he could trust regardless of how meaningless the task.

"Wallace, I want you to check out Angela's home at 245 Sand Hill Lane," Nathan announced into his radiophone in hopes that he would answer.

"On my way, Sir, I'll call you as soon as I have something to report."

"Bring the baby back, and quietly dispose of Angela Gibbs. No witnesses."

"You know me, Sir. This is what I live for. I'll call you when it's done."

"I await your call."

Wallace hung up the receiver. He looked around to see where he was in location to the address Nathan gave him. Wallace was too far, he had to turn around and head back. While Wallace checked out this last lead, Nathan was hell bent in getting other avenues started, but first he had to have his office cleaned.

"Send Security to my office now," Nathan said, speaking into an intercom. Two Security Guards immediately reported for duty. They looked down at Sawyer lying dead on the floor, but didn't move a muscle until Nathan gave them their orders. Although Nathan could make a small fortune on the black market by having Sawyer carted off for dissection, he needed to make an example of him so that no one else would lose control and violate protocol.

"Throw his carcass to the vultures and make certain that he can't be identified in any way. When you've done that send in Agent Reynolds," Nathan barked. The security guards picked up the body, and headed out the door. On their way out to put the body in the truck they see Agent Reynolds and inform him to see Nathan Anderson.

"Hey, Reynolds, Nathan wants to see you right away," the security guard announced. Agent Reynolds just nodded his head in the affirmative as he stopped in his tracks and gasped while he watched them carry away his dead boss to who knows where. He then continued walking, looking more worried with each step.

***

As Wallace drove down the street headed towards Angela's home. Angela and the baby pass him going the opposite direction. Angela's car was packed full of stuff. Wallace didn't see her pass by, as he was too intent on watching for street names and house numbers. He pulled up in the driveway and entered the house. It was completely empty. He looked about for anything that could give him some clue as to where they went. There wasn't even a 'for sale' sign out in the yard. Wallace radioed back to Nathan the bad news.

"Anderson," Nathan answered. His manner was quite gruff, and in his gut he knew what Wallace had to report.

"She's gone, sir. There's not a trace of her, or the baby. This was a well thought out plan."

Nathan hung up the radio receiver and lit another cigarette. He took a slow, long, deliberate drag on the coffin nail that he held firmly between his index and middle fingers. His lungs filled with the flavorful smoke until he reached that moment of precise fullness that satisfied his need without coughing. The crackling sound of incinerating tobacco leaves and paper was, for a brief moment, the only sound in the room. This moment of enjoyment was all that Nathan would know for a while, and although brief, tried to relish it as along as he could. Reynolds finally arrived at Nathan's office with great trepidation in his demeanor and voice.

"You wanted to see me sir?" Reynolds questioned with sober politeness. He could see the wheels churning behind Nathan's icy stare. Although his eyes had not yet met Reynolds' gaze, Reynolds knew that Nathan was deep in contemplation of an action plan to secure the lost property or engage upon a major cover up.

"Yes, you've just been promoted. Find that woman, eliminate her, and bring back my property. I sent Wallace out to her home. It's completely empty."

"I'll get right on it," Reynolds acknowledged. He hesitated because he could see that Nathan hadn't actually dismissed him yet. In his present mood he didn't want to push him any further over the edge.

"I need that baby to complete our genetic experiments. I want results. Do you hear me? Results!" Nathan exclaimed emphasizing his words with a fist to his desk. The desk was struck so hard that his ashtray, penholders, and things literally jumped off the desk tossing some ash upon the desktop.

"Sir, I've been going over her methods. This heist was well thought out. I will, however, exhaust every avenue available to us. Although my gut tells me, we won't find much."

"We can't afford another mistake. No one can find out what we're doing here, or if we can't get her back, what we've lost."

"I don't intend to make a mistake, but I …"

"Why are you belaboring this?" Nathan questioned, sharply.

"Because, I don't want to end up like my boss when the odds are against us succeeding."

"Just get busy. So long as you are investigating every avenue and covering up the error, I'll not kill you for not finding her. Although if you do find her and lose her again, I will."

***

The guards arrived in the middle of the desert. They had already stripped the body of all clothing and identification. Sawyer's fingertips were bloody as they were cut off back at the lab. They gruffly pulled the body out of the back of the truck and tossed it on the ground like a sack of dirty laundry. One of the guards grabbed a hammer out of the back of the truck, knelt down, raised the hammer up, and followed through striking out his teeth and bone to make a positive ID impossible should the skeletal remains ever be found. After the teeth had been knocked out, they gathered them in a sack to be disposed of back at the labs. Before leaving they covered the body in Coyote bait so that the animals would quickly eat the carcass leaving the bones to bake in the desert sun.

Prairie Lights was inspired by the loss of wonder that seems to plague our society. There are many things in our universe that can't be explained. The subject of the Marfa Lights of Texas has always intrigued me. They have received a lot of notoriety over the years and some are convinced that the mysterious lights floating above the prairie are explained as headlights from cars in the distance. However, they go back much father than that explanation. In addition, other phenomena accompany the true Marfa Lights such as high pitched sounds before they appear. I'm not a big proponent of little green men, but I'm very much about remembering that we live in a grand and marvelous universe. Sometimes, it's not about knowing how it works. It's about appreciating the beauty in it.

PRAIRIE LIGHTS

Two students from a nearby university arrive at the log cabin of Diane Stanton just outside the Marfa, TX city limits to observe the Marfa Lights. Mrs. Stanton, a widow and single mother of her only daughter, Stella, were pleased to have the university students come. Their home's location made for the best scientific observations of the mysterious lights, and the university always paid Mrs. Stanton a handsome sum for the use of her home. The two students this time were two males finishing their graduate studies. They had arrived in a Hummer, the property of the man driving. Mrs. Stanton came out of the house to greet them.

"Hello, gentlemen, I'm Mrs. Stanton. You two must be from the university."

"Yes, I'm Scott Hutchins, and this is Terry Trevor."

"I have the guest room ready for you. You can set up your equipment on the back porch."

"Thank you," Scott acknowledged. Terry just nodded and proceeded to unload their vast array of scientific equipment. Suddenly, a ten-year old girl came running up to the two men just as bold as she could be.

"You're here to figure out the lights aren't ya?"

"Yes, we are, and who might you be?"

"I'm Stella."

"Hello, Stella, I'm Scott. That ugly guy over there is Terry."

Terry just gave a perturbed look back at Scott, and nodded hello to the little girl. The two had been roommates for nearly four years now, and had become more like brothers than just friends.

"You boys brought and awful lot of stuff just to go back empty handed," Stella commented.

"What makes you think we'll go back empty handed?"

"What makes you think you're smarter than anybody else that's come up here?"

"Stella!" her mom scolded.

"It's ok Mrs. Stanton. I like a bold half pint."

"Hey, I'm not a half pint. I'm ten years old."

"Well, I'm twenty years old and that make you a half pint."

Stella put her hands on her hips and pouted for just a moment, but then decided she would accept this nickname. Her acceptance was clear by a grin that cascaded across her freckled face. Her long stringy red hair and dirt on the knees of her blue jeans was a sure sign that this spitfire young lady was a Tomboy. Scott then tossed her a lighter piece of equipment for her to carry that she caught like an expert ball player.

"Come on, I'll take you out back," Stella conceded. Scott just smiled at his buddy Terry and followed the little girl around the back of the house. Her mom looked on, and was satisfied that Stella had made a friend.

Later that night it was completely dark with no moonlight. The only light came from the stars scattered along the black velvet sky above providing just a faint glow on the plains below them. Scott and Terry were a little jittery wondering if the lights would appear that night. It was a prime observation opportunity but a naturally occurring phenomenon doesn't always oblige new observers with their presence.

Stella came out onto the porch as quietly as a tiny mouse. Scott and Terry were way too engrossed in their work to notice her. Stella got a mischievous idea, and allowed the screen door to slam. Both men nearly jumped out of their skins.

"Sweet …" Scott stammered as he nearly knocked over his camera.

"You little squirt," Terry commented.

"The name is half pint. You ain't gonna scare them away if you make a noise," Stella announced.

"How do you know?"

"I live here, remember."

"Oh yeah. All right, if you're so smart, are we going to see one tonight?"

"The Prairie Sprites will be here in a few minutes, right over there," Stella announced, pointing over the horizon beyond a tree line toward the south.

"Prairie Sprites?"

"That's what mama calls them."

"You seem pretty sure of yourself."

"Yes, she is," Mrs. Stanton interrupted. Scott immediately stood to his feet just like his mother taught him when a woman enters a room.

"Mrs. Stanton."

"I made you boys some coffee. These observations usually take all night."

"Thank you," Terry added, taking the warm cup from her.

"I'm curious as to how Stella is so certain where they'll appear," Scott inquired.

"I'll be damned," Terry announced interrupting Mrs. Stanton's response to the question. "There they are, just where the girl said."

Scott immediately jumped to his equipment checking readings, and taking pictures. They were monitoring infrared and other spectrums to determine the entire range of the Marfa lights. The little girl smiled with pride.

"They'll sing in just a bit."

"Sing?" Scott questioned.

"Whoa, what was that? Scott, did you hear something?" Terry asked.

"Yes, I did."

"They're sad tonight. The sound is uncomfortable only when they're sad," Stella informed. Scott looked up from his equipment and looked over at Stella. Then he turned back around to find the lights gone.

"Where'd they go?"

"They'll be back in just a few minutes. They didn't like that area. They'll be going over there next."

"Look!" Terry announced with jubilation as another cluster of lights began to appear again just where the girl said they would. They began to dance and twinkle. It was beautiful to watch. The students' reactions were like watching two youngsters in a toyshop filled with all their favorites. Mrs. Stanton smiled as she watched them for a few moments.

"Stella, it's time for bed."

"Ah, mom. Can't I stay up a little while longer?"

"No, you have school tomorrow."

"But they might need my help."

"We'll be okay, half pint. Now go do what your mother says. We'll still be here in the morning."

"Good night."

"Good night, half pint."

Mrs. Stanton put her daughter to bed and then rejoined the young men a few minutes later. She, too, had a cup of coffee when she emerged from the house and took a seat on her porch swing. She noticed the men discussing a technical problem amongst themselves.

"You boys having some problems?"

"Don't know. It looks like the equipment is working, but it's not doing much," Scott answered. Mrs. Stanton just smiled.

"The lights are very elusive. You're not the first group to be disappointed by what they didn't learn."

"You stood up for you daughter when I questioned her confidence level about where and when the lights would show up. I think there's more to that statement then what was said."

"You pick up on subtlety rather well Mr. Hutchins."

"Would you care to elaborate?"

"I would. About six years ago, my late husband and I went camping about twenty miles in that direction. Jason would always take us out into the middle of the prairie to look at the stars. You can see so much beauty out there." Diane paused for a moment. Scott and Terry could see that it was a fond remembrance and that her heart still belonged to her husband.

"Please go on, you describe it so nicely that it makes me want to take up astronomy."

"I'm sorry, I still miss Jason. In any case, Stella was only four then and she had wandered off chasing some lightning bugs. All of a sudden Jason and I realized that Stella was nowhere to be found. We called and called, and no answer. We called the authorities. They sent out search parties, but she was gone.

The police convinced us to go on home and they would let us know as soon as they located her."

"I can't imagine how frightened you were, but you obviously found her."

"Actually, no one found her. She showed up on our back porch the next day. Believe me when I tell you that there is no way a four-year-old little girl can wander ten plus miles through the prairie in the middle of the night and live to tell about it. The coyotes should have gotten her, but there she was. When we asked her how she made it home she said the Prairie Sprites brought her home, and kept the coyotes at bay."

"That's an incredible story."

"Yes. It's so incredible that my own family called me a liar. I maybe many things, but I've never been a liar. Whether you believe the lights were a providence of God set forth to bring back my baby girl, a friendly alien, or some specter matters little to me. That they brought back my baby does matter. She has a keen awareness of them Mr. Hutchins. I'm glad they were there. Jason used to say that the earth is full of wonders that were never meant for man to dissect and analyze, but to enjoy them for the beauty that they are."

"Your husband was a wise man."

"Yes, if you boys will excuse me. I've got an early day tomorrow, and don't be too disappointed in what you don't learn about the Marfa lights. As long as you appreciate them, then their purpose in the cosmos is fulfilled. Goodnight gentlemen."

"Goodnight Mrs. Stanton," Terry acknowledged.

"Now there goes a true woman."

"Yes, indeed. Now are we going to study these things or not?" Terry questioned.

"Let's get to studying."

The next morning Scott and Terry were awakened by the smell of pancakes and bacon. The smell was extremely alluring to these grad students who have only had limited exposure to such good down home cooking. Stella skipped down the hallway toward the dining room. Her long stringy red hair was now neatly combed and braided. She was wearing tailored, navy blue pants, and a pressed white blouse with the emblem of her school on the left side. Scott and Terry had fallen asleep in their clothes on the porch and were yawning and stretching as they made their way to the breakfast table.

"That smells so good," Scott mentioned as he pulled up a chair to the table that was set for four.

"Being university students I figured that your access to good home cooking was limited."

"Indeed, it is. Thank you for going to such trouble for us."

"No trouble, it does me good to fix for others."

"Did you get what you came for?" Stella asked, all bright-eyed.

"Well, we got lots of data. Whether that gives us what we came here for or not, I don't know."

"Don't be surprised if you come up empty handed."

"Why?"

"Because everybody else does."

"Why do you suppose that is half pint?"

"Mama says that God puts some things in this world, not for us to understand, but to appreciate the magic of life."

"Your mama's a wise woman."

Promised Land was actually the beginning to a new novel, but the idea never fully materialized. It's not the encouraging story like Prairie Lights. It is, however, a testament to how life can change in an instant. There are a multitude of examples throughout history and in our contemporary society that play out everyday. It's a reminder that our status; both socially and economically, as well as our freedom, is a daily gift to be treasured. Why? Because it could all disappear in a moment.

PROMISED LAND

Josiah awoke in a cold sweat from his dream-laden sleep. He looked over his shoulder to make certain that his parents were still there, and with a sigh of relief rolled back over hoping the rest of the night would let him sleep without the frightening images of the events that had unfolded just a month ago.

He remembered so clearly sitting at the dinner table discussing with his parents what he wanted to do for his tenth birthday. His father had promised him a camping trip along the Amethyst River just the three of them. It was a trip that was never going to be for that same evening soldiers forced their way into the house and arrested both of his parents. Josiah was horrified. His father had done nothing wrong, and was a Senator in the Unified Alliance Government. The president, Elbert Rothmere, had given his father, Thomas, the highest commendation a citizen could receive the previous year. The soldiers had charged him and his mother, Louise with heresy and treason.

Josiah recalled his petition to release his parents telling the soldiers that they were making a mistake. He even ran to the mantle where his father's commendation was displayed and pushed it into the faces of the soldiers. One of them kicked him, but he got right back up to defend his parents. They wound up taking all three of them to a military installation where they kept him locked up in a room by himself for several days. He wasn't sure how many days, but when he was reunited with his mother she had been beaten so much that he could not hug her because it hurt her too badly to do so. He wept that night staying as close as he could without touching her wondering if she would die. Her face was bruised and swollen, and she herself had reached a point where there were no tears left to cry. He tried at one point to hold her hand, but even her fingers were bruised.

After a few more days, his mother began to recover. Conditions, however, were horrid. They were given moldy bread to eat and dirty water to drink. Their cell smelled from their own waste because there were no facilities given to them for waste removal. Thinking back he wondered how they ever lived through it. They were kept in the dark with the exception of what sunlight filtered through a small skylight high in the ceiling. Information about his father was non-existent. He could see the fear in his mother's eyes. There was something going on much more terrible than what had directly affected his family, but Louise wouldn't talk about it with her son. She did her best to keep his hope alive focusing upon when the three of them would be together again.

Josiah didn't want to upset her so he never told her that he didn't believe they would ever see his father again. Much to his surprise the day before his birthday soldiers came to their cell and took them to yet another facility. It was there that they were reunited with Thomas. His father had also been beaten and tortured. His shirt had been ripped and through the tears one could see the impressions of the whip that had cut into his back. His father apologized for not being able to take him on his camping trip, but Josiah didn't care about the camping trip anymore. He had his parents back, and knew that was the best and only present he could get.

Through all of their trials, none of them knew why this had happened to them until his birthday the next day. That morning they, along with hundreds and at times seemed like thousands of people, were herded into a large arena. A huge video screen had been set up, and soon an image of President Elbert Rothmere appeared before them. He made an elaborate speech on how he was justified in taking control of the Unified Alliance Government. How he abolished the Senate and how anyone who had opposed him on any issue was now in custody as a political prisoner.

He claimed that his way was the only way to restore law and order to the Alliance and was not going to be stopped by a Senate who didn't have the courage to make the tough decisions. Then he went on to prove to the people that he was not seizing control as a ruthless dictator, but as a visionary whose only purpose was to make the Unified Alliance a paradise for its citizens. This proof would be that he would have mercy on these political prisoners as well as the criminals of their society. Instead of executions or imprisonment, he was sending them all to the planet of Crestfallen. Crestfallen was an undeveloped wilderness with harsh seasons. It had been declared uninhabitable by their standards, but to the general populace was being presented as the Promised Land where these misguided citizens could live with their own philosophy without sacrificing the rest of the Alliance.

A planetary trip was not cheap, but he showed on many graphs and charts how in the long run it would be cheaper to banish those prisoners rather than supporting them through the prison system. As he put it with his new age thinking, prisons would be a thing of the past. Those that were not interested or were a threat to the well being of the whole would be sent to Crestfallen where they would be too busy in just living to create division or anarchy.

Josiah remembered the terrified looks of his parents after the president's announcement, but before he could question them about what the president had said they were immediately herded into a tunnel where they were stripped of their current clothing with no regard for their dignity. They were hosed down with a mixture of soap, water, and antiseptics. At the end of the tunnel they were handed a brown pair of pants and a tunic. One size fits all. If you were small, it looked like a tent. If you were big, you were uncomfortable. They were handed one canteen of water each, and a pouch filled with dehydrated foodstuffs.

After that they were paraded before the cameras documenting the compassion of the new government as they boarded the Unified Alliance Government Ship Rancor. They stood elbow to elbow with hardcore criminals as well as other political prisoners. The ship had many compartments and families were secured together in spaces no bigger than a closet. His parents were propped up against the wall to provide enough room for him to lie down and sleep. Part of him hoped he would never sleep again, and part hoped that he could sleep just once without the nightmares. Here on Crestfallen life and death played out every moment. How he longed for the safety of all his yesterdays. The people around him were a people without a vision or a hope, and without a hope the people perish.

The Perfect Moment was inspired by a real life event, but so much of what it inspired is still unfinished. It has been challenged as a fake, but I believe that it was real. More than that I believe that its true power was found in what it bestowed upon those that remained earthbound. We've become so technologically savvy that we forget that the first moon landing was less about technology and more about human ingenuity, hard work, and unwavering bravery than anything else. It was an endeavor that was a tribute to the human spirit, blessed by God, and did more for world peace than any other act. Through exploration of the universe peace could be achieved. Apollo-Soyuz missions were a testimony to what could be during a time when the Iron curtain separated two peoples that at one time were allies. It became a proof that hope still remained. In our current world climate where the Iron Curtain and the Berlin Wall are a thing of the past, it should remind us that terrorism must not snuff out our beacon of hope. We must stay the course and see it through.

In many ways this experience related through this poem has been my hearts cry in life and has influenced all my work. It sustained me when the Space Shuttle Challenger exploded and its cloud hovered in the sky for hours after the fatal accident and reminded me that the pursuit of knowledge can be just as costly as ignorance.

THE PERFECT MOMENT

When I was a child there was one perfect moment that the whole world knew.
I sat spellbound to the television as a man walked on the moon.
I sat completely still, nor did I dare breathe.
An impossible dream had been made reality.

In that moment the world stopped in time.
Together looked on at this wondrous sight.
No classes, or race, in that moment of clarity.
Centuries of hate melted in space.

An accomplishment rode to the moon that day,
One of peace whose taste was so very sweet.
"Can't" died on this day.
Tomorrow was sure to bring a brighter way.

If we could go to the moon, we could do anything.
We could love our neighbor, feed the poor, and heal the sick.
And close the door of injustice for good.

This single moment has never grown bitter,
Nor faded in my heart all together.
Daily I strive to prepare the way,
When all of our moments will unfold in this way.

First Published by Quill Books, "A Time to Be Free" ©1999 ISBN 0-943536-72-3

LIFE

A Love for More Than A Season, is about two people who share a lifetime together without regret. In so much of our cinema and literature love stories belong to the young and usually center around their sexual exploits. Real love is about so much more than that. I was inspired by the marriages in my family that have lasted for fifty and sixty plus years. My own has lasted 27 years and is better than ever. I've always said you want to show me love, don't show me newlyweds show me an elderly couple that still holds hands with each other. Those that have been through the ups and downs of life and have come through the other side stronger for it are those that have shared a lifetime and still choose to love the partner they began the journey with. Until death do us part, is not the beginning of a fantasy, but of a journey. Lifetime relationships don't just happen they are work for both partners and the most powerful tool any couple can employ is forgiveness and acceptance.

A LOVE FOR MORE THAN A SEASON

A long procession of cars weaved its way down a coastal highway. An elderly man was riding in the back looking at the ocean from his seat. He was a frail old man dressed in his Sunday best. He sat tall and straight holding his cane between his knees.

"Stop here," the old man demanded of the driver.

"Here, sir?" the young driver asked.

"Yes, here," the old man confirmed. The driver complied and pulled off to the side. He got out and opened the door to assist the old man up to his feet.

"I can do this myself," he insisted refusing his help.

The younger man backed away. The old man stood up straight now that he had his balance and straightened his jacket. He surveyed the beach and carefully shuffled down the embankment of the road. With carefully placed steps he waded through sea oats and salt marsh grass until finally he emerged upon the white sandy shore. The sun beat down upon his skin so warm and bright. His eye caught a colorful seashell. He knelt down on one knee to retrieve the small treasure. In a moment he was transported back in time when he was handsome and strong and was nervously gazing in wonder at the girl of his dreams. It was right there on the beach that he asked her to the school dance then later to be his wife.

She became the joy of his life and they got married only a few yards from where he was that very moment. It wasn't a large wedding just a few family and friends. Their honeymoon was also spent here. They didn't have much money back then, but that didn't matter. This beach was paradise to he and his wife and took almost every dime they had to pay the rent. Those first years were simple, but they were happy and content. At times there were clouds that gathered, but together they always made it through.

His eyes, now faded, looked down the way and saw a boarded up shack about to give way. Yet all he could recall was a man selling corn dogs and ice cream. The breeze blew against his pant leg, and he remembered his small young son's hand and voice begging for a cone.

A scent blew by from the ocean side. A fish fry was conjured up by this shifting wind when his oldest graduated from school way back then. There were kids and laughter, songs and food, smiles that would linger all night long. The waves that slapped upon the sand became the splashes and giggles of a precious grandchild that fit in his hand.

The old man stood to his feet once more brushing the sand from his knee. How quick and precious was life through these eyes, but the youthful reflection seemed longer somehow. Footprints in the sand washed away by a wave. He had no regrets, nor remorse for a love both faithful and brave. He hummed an old tune that comforted his heart, and then another familiar love, came and took hold of his arm.

"Dad, we need to go," a young woman invited. His daughter, how much she now looks like her mother. Her smile was always the key to this daddy's heart.

"Yes, you're right," he smiled. He carefully placed the seashell in his pocket and walked with his grown daughter back to the car. They continued on to their destination.

Family and friends from many generations were gathered together. There were songs sang and stories recited, but it wasn't long enough to celebrate his true love's life. The service was over and people departed, but the old man stayed a while before parting. A single tear fell down his face, but was met with a smile of timeless grace. While some left flowers in memory of his love, he left a seashell for his one true love. There are those who cling to the emptiness of death, but he chose to cling to the gift of love they shared in this life.

The Forgotten was inspired by my love for the men and women who serve in our military. My family has served in wartime and in peace in all branches of the service. Currently my daughter's boyfriend is an active duty marine serving overseas. We all support our troops and cheer for them. We pray for their safety, and we mourn their loss when they've given the ultimate sacrifice. There is a group that is many times forgotten, the wounded and the aged veterans. Those that come home, but not the same way they left. Many face huge challenges that the cheering crowds aren't there to encourage. This is a reminder to support these families in their time of need.

The Forgotten

Jennifer Grant was sitting in her living room drowning her sorrows in a pint of Rocky Road ice cream. She was fifty-five today, and her husband had been dead six months come Tuesday. Their two grown children, Rachel who attends college out of state, and Jared, who was way closer to being a hippie than she had ever come, had forgotten her birthday. Unless of course you count Jared's dirty laundry that he brings to his mother like clockwork every other week. Her and her late husband's best friends took Jennifer out to dinner, but the absence of her husband, Rick, amid the foursome was too much for her to bear so she left early.

She played with the ice cream as it melted watching it drip. Part of her was angry toward everybody including Rick. How could he leave her like this? She had so much on her plate, and no one seemed to care. Her children were too busy with their own social lives to even check on her or be troubled to pick up the phone and wish her a happy birthday. Then there was the matter of all those apartments that needed renovating. Rick was going to fix them up and rent them out, but he never got that chance. She didn't know the first thing about how to fix things up so she placed an ad for a handyman. No one, however, had applied for the job and it had been in the paper for a week already. Somewhere amid her self-pity she drifted off to sleep.

Jennifer was awakened the next morning by a loud knocking on the door. Not having gone to bed the night before she looked awful. Her makeup was still on at least what didn't get washed away by her tears, and her mouth had chocolate stains in the corners. She stood up and walked to the door. To her surprise stood a handsome man in his late thirties to early forties dressed in a military uniform.

"May I help you?" she asked squinting the sun from her eyes.

"Are you Mrs. Grant?" he inquired.

"Yes," she answered, primping slightly.

"My name is Kyle Coffman. I've come in answer to your ad for a handyman. I was hoping you hadn't filled the position."

"But you're in the Marines."

"Was, Ma'am, I was discharged. Your ad mentioned that you would provide room and board."

"Yes."

"Ma'am, are you okay?"

"Yesterday was my birthday."

"That must have been some party."

"You have no idea, Gunny."

"How'd you know that I was a Gunny?"

"My dad. Follow me."

Kyle followed her around the back of the house to where the apartments stood with windows boarded up. In the back was a small efficiency that they used to use for Rick's mom.

"I've brought some references if you want to see them," he offered.

"That won't be necessary. Your ribbons tell me everything I need to know. It's a little dusty in here, but everything works. I'll bring you some fresh linens for the bed and towels."

"When would you like me to start?"

"Tomorrow. I'll let you get settled in. Then I'll take you on a tour of the complex and give you an inventory of what supplies and tools we currently have on hand. Then you tell me what we have to purchase, the order the repairs need to be done in, and if you'll require any help with any of the repairs."

"Fair enough."

"I'll fetch your linens."

"Mrs. Grant."

"Yes?"

"Happy Birthday."

"Thank you."

Over the next couple weeks Jennifer and Kyle got a chance to know one another. Although Kyle was a good fifteen years her junior, you couldn't tell as Jennifer was a beautiful woman who looked much younger than her chronological age. The more he was around the happier she was. She even caught herself dressing up and fixing her face more than she usually did. Even though the wisdom of her fifty-five years told her that he probably would never be interested in a woman as old as she, Jennifer was still a woman. She had almost forgot the simple joy of having a man around the house to talk to.

One day it was particularly warm so she made some lemonade and took it out to him. He was busy hammering when he noticed her standing there with the glass of cold refreshment. She held it out to him with a schoolgirl's smile. He gladly took it from her. Their fingers touched briefly during the exchange. Her heart fluttered. She quickly inhaled and blushed as if her entire emotion towards him was laid bare. He smiled noticing the gleam in her eye, but paid little attention to the blush. The sun was so hot that he mistook it for the body's natural reaction to the heat dismissing it out of hand. He did, however, notice how beautiful she looked.

"Thank you Mrs. Grant."

"Please, call me Jennifer," she pleaded. "My husband has been dead a little over six months now."

"That explains it."

"Explains what?"

"How a woman as beautiful as you is living alone."

"Thank you," she said blushing, again. "You don't have to say that. A man of your age, well. In any case, my husband bought these apartments and he was going to fix them up and rent them out, but died of a massive heart attack before he could even start."

"I'm sorry for your loss."

"My husband wasn't even unhealthy. It was just one of those things…" Jennifer started to tear up, but turned around to reclaim her sensibilities.

Kyle gently put his hand upon her shoulder to provide her some comfort. He knew what it was like to lose men who had your back in battle; but he could only imagine what it must be like to lose someone you loved. Someone who made you feel that no matter where you were – so long as you were together you were home.

"I truly am sorry for your loss, and yes a man of my age does find you very beautiful."

"Do you have a family?" she asked, trying to change the subject from herself.

"No, I was married once, but she couldn't take the deployments and divorced me before we had children. I didn't try again. Do you have children?"

"Two, although you'd never realize it. Since their father died, they never call unless they need money or laundry. My daughter's in college and my son thinks he's Picasso."

"Give them time. Kid's cope with things in their own way."

"But I feel so forgotten."

"Sounds to me like you've lost your way." Jennifer just shrugged her shoulders to Kyle's comment. "I'm going to visit some people this Saturday. I'd like for you to accompany me."

"Why?"

"Because I enjoy your company, and I think the people that I'm going to visit will also enjoy your company. Besides it'll do you good to get out of the house and your routine. I'll even spring for dinner with no strings attached, just two people enjoying great food and conversation."

"What should I wear?" she asked. His smile broadened across his face with her acceptance.

"Something comfortable and pretty."

"And time?"

"Be ready at o' nine hundred."

"Yes, Sir," she answered with a mock salute.

Saturday was a beautiful day. The sky was clear and sunny and Jennifer was ready to go at 9:00 a.m. Kyle was dressed in a nice pair of dungarees with a white cotton top that accentuated his muscles. She wore the latest fashion jeans and colorful top that brought modest definition to a still beautiful figure. Jennifer still didn't know where they were going and was quite shocked when Kyle drove up into the parking lot of a Veterans Administration Hospital. Seeing the lost expression upon her face Kyle began to explain.

"Ever since I joined the Marines, wherever I'm stationed, if there is a V.A. Hospital within driving distance I come every Saturday to visit those that for whatever reason don't or can't have visitors."

"What do you mean by can't have visitors?"

"Some of the veterans are elderly and their spouses and immediate families are no longer living."

"I had no idea. And the others?"

"The others are young servicemen and women who have been wounded and require extensive treatments before returning home. It's too expensive to house their spouses and children all those weeks."

"That's awful. Why doesn't someone do something about it?"

"Some do, but it's not enough. Most of the time they're forgotten."

"That's so sad."

"That's true, some of these situations are quite sad. We're not here to add to that. We're here to lift their spirits."

"Understood."

Kyle parked the car. Jennifer got out and followed his lead. They reached a room where soldiers who suffered some of the more severe injuries were recovering. Her first reaction was to break down into tears, but then she recalled Kyle's words. She also remembered visiting her own father when he was convalescing from wounds sustained in Viet Nam. She breathed deeply and forced a great bright smile across her face accompanying Kyle from bedside to bedside. Kyle introduced her to one soldier who was near and dear to his heart.

"Jennifer, I'd like for you to meet, Lance Corporal Roberts. He served under me in Afghanistan, and saved my life."

"I'm pleased to meet you, Lance Corporal Roberts."

"Well you're too beautiful and young to be Gunny's mom or sister. How did you meet?" Roberts asked. He was pretty jovial considering that he had no legs from the knees down.

"I'm his employer, actually, but we've become good friends."

"If you don't mind, I'm going to let you two get acquainted I see some new familiar faces," Kyle said excusing himself.

"So tell me Lance Corporal, how does a fine Marine like you end up in a place like this?"

"Well, if we were stateside you'd always find us in a V.A. Hospital. Kyle demanded it of us. Before we went off to play we would come and visit. He said that it was putting deposits in for a time when we would need to make a withdrawal. I'm making one hell of a withdrawal. My story is no different than any other. An I.E.D. which we noticed two seconds too late went off. I pushed Kyle down. Skittles, he was toast. I don't think we found much of anything save his head and dog tags, and me, well my legs went on a one-way ticket to Timbuktu. I just wish I could see my wife and kids. They're up in Oregon and I'm down here in Tampa Bay."

"Tell me about your wife."

"She's a beautiful brunette. Got a smile that will just light up a room. How she ever fell in love with a guy like me? I'll never know, but she did and she is as true as they come."

"And your kids?"

"Oh, I've got two boys, six and four they are so smart and good at sports. The six year old is in Pee Wee Football and the four year old is in Tee Ball. I got pictures," he offered. Roberts grabbed his cell phone and began showing off his brood. Jennifer looked through the photos and could see the pride and love exuding from him. It reminded her of the love and pride Rick had in them years ago.

"Will you excuse me a moment?" Jennifer asked. She went to seek out a hospital administrator. She inquired about Roberts' condition and about how long he would need to remain there before he could be sent home to his family. They were hesitant at first until she divulged that she wanted to provide housing free of charge for Roberts' family. She also inquired of the hospital about any other extreme cases that she may not be aware of that would need temporary housing and how long.

After a while Kyle noticed that Jennifer wasn't in the main room where the visitors were at, and he started looking for her. When she finally came back into the room she was beaming a great smile. He was curious as to what happened that changed since their arrival at the hospital. He tried to question her there, but she refused saying that she would share over dinner. They completed their visit, but not until Jennifer finished reading a chapter of a book to a man who had lost his sight. She promised him that she would be back next week to read again.

At a sidewalk café they enjoyed an early dinner. She questioned him about how long it would take him to complete the apartment he was currently working on. Then she divulged her plans to use it for Roberts' family at no cost to them. Kyle stopped eating and began to weep.

"I thought you'd be pleased."

"I'm more than pleased. I'm moved. You were so good with the patients, but I never dreamed that you'd…"

"I'm not done. I plan on launching my own campaign because I won't be able to sustain it without community support. I'm calling it 'Operation Remember' and Roberts' family will be the first. I already spoke to the hospital administrator. They're making arrangements for them to be here by next Saturday. So we've got a lot of work to do."

"Yes Ma'am," Kyle saluted. She smiled. He then reached over and kissed her like she hadn't been kissed in a very long time.

Next Saturday arrived. Kyle and Jennifer picked up Roberts' family from the airport and brought them to the V.A. Hospital. When they walked into the Lance Corporal's room, he was so moved that he couldn't contain the tears of joy. His boys ran to his side and climbed upon his bed like they were climbing a tree. His wife kissed him repeatedly while Kyle and Jennifer looked on. They slipped out quietly to give them a family moment. Jennifer was beaming a great smile. Kyle looked over at her.

"This is what a birthday should feel like!" she exclaimed as she hugged him.

My Name Is Love was written to celebrate the birth of a friend's child. At the time we had very little money to buy a gift for this occasion so I gave my gift of writing to them. I sat down one afternoon to compose a celebration of this new life, printed it on baby themed paper, and framed it. Because it was a gift from the heart it was cherished by this couple, just as much or more than the more expensive gifts they received.

MY NAME IS LOVE

My name is love, a gift from God above.

Conceived in love a miracle to hold, and
A treasure more precious than silver or gold.

In my eyes the light of heaven burns clear and bright.
My laughter is the song of angels in the morning light.

To your arms I will take my very first steps,
And in those arms you'll comfort my failed attempts.

Teach me obedience and faith in the Lord with a firm and caring hand.
So when it is my turn to face the world, I too can stand.

We will have seasons of joy and seasons of pain.
Yet, all will be better by love shown simply and plain.

When I am sick you will stand guard over my bed.
Praise be in the morning when I am well again!

You will come to know love like you have never known.
It is special and grand for a lifetime to come.

Though I may have traditions, titles and carry your name.
I will always be love, a gift from God above.

The Futility of Hate was inspired by my hatred of prejudice and injustice. I was born in 1963 just three months before J.F.K. was assassinated. My young eyes watched riots, protests, and the violence that came when people refused to grant others who were different simple basic human rights. It made me ill to watch and I made a promise to myself that I would never judge anyone on the basis of race, or anything else. I would offer my respect to those around me and I would teach my children the same.

I passed my respect for others down to my children. I don't allow disrespect in private or in public. Neither will I stand idly by while someone else is treated improperly. As an example, my daughter recently befriended a Muslim girl at the college she attends. In the face of ridicule by the girls she had been previously sitting with, my daughter defended her. When the other girls continued to make snide comments about her being different, my daughter got up and ate her lunch at another table with the Muslim girl. Talking they discovered that they had more in common than they initially thought. They were also very much aware that in the Muslim girl's homeland that a Jew sitting with a Muslim would not be accepted. I was very proud of her. My daughter not only made a new friend, together they are breaking down barriers which society in its ignorance has built.

THE FUTILITY OF HATE

Hate has never built anything of honor to behold.
Its place is the barriers and stumbling blocks of old.
It cannot stand with another for it abhors all beside itself.
Hate is deaf, dumb, and blind whose council is itself.

It is a poison that is learned and passed to another.
A disease that destroys those it touches and its carrier.
It is a worm that eats away at the soul.
Hate is a stench both vile and foul.

It is man's worst sin and shame to all.
Yet love can overcome this terrible flaw.
There is nothing as strong as one who loves,
That which is different just because.

A legacy of love is for all,
Love cannot be kept inside a wall.
For love to conquer this thing called hate,
It must be loosed from inside the gate.

First published in "The Harvest of Dreams" © 2001 Int'l Library of Poetry ISBN# 0-7951-5040-7
Second time published in "Writers For Relief" © 2005 ISBN# 1-4116-5682-2

Like the Willow was birthed during a very difficult time in my own life. It was a time I felt like a failure. Throughout my life I've turned to writing to express my feelings and to relieve the weightiness of my heart. Perhaps you, too, have found yourself in such a place, but just like the night that gives way to day. The pain will eventually give way to joy. My pain did give way to joy, and I hope that you will find strength in knowing that if someone has felt pain this deeply and emerged joyous. Then hope remains for your situation also.

LIKE THE WILLOW

I cried myself to sleep last night,
As I wrestle against my demons.
A tortured heart seems my eternal plight,
To find the love I've needed.

Too long I have poured myself out for nothing in return.
Tears too many to number have fallen to the ground.
Hurts so deep that they haunt my steps begging me to turn
To protect my heart, but still I yearn.

I look this way and that trying to find the path,
That's free from guilt, pain, and wrath.
I seek a love that's tried and true,
Filled with trust that strengthens two.

Burdened with worries and so much strife.
How can I continue to be a wife?
A broken spirit cannot continue in this life
As an empty vessel tossed aside.

Right or wrong, left or right,
Too many choices to make in just one night.
As I wipe my silent tears away, and lay my head upon my pillow.
I'm sure I'll continue to weep, just like the willow.

Memories was inspired by fond recollections of my youth and family. These ideas and philosophies was imparted to me by the examples lived by my grandparents, parents, aunts, and uncles. It is a collection of their most graceful attributes all rolled into one.

MEMORIES

Memories are the threads of the tapestry that is our life.
Simple treasures of love hover close to the hearth.
Small pains of hard lessons learned that stoked the fire of our growth,
Which exposed the futility of idle strife.

The threads of laughter bring joy in sorrow and warmth for the cold.
Giggles of delight are a bright light for the night.
Cherished smiles of approval for things done right.
Are treasure more perfect than silver or gold.

It is these things that make a house a home.
But most important is the heart where Christ is Lord.
For in him all things good richly abound.
And his house will remain a refuge by those whose love made it a home.

First Published by Quill Books, "A Time to Be Free" ©1999 ISBN 0-943536-72-3

Price of Freedom is by far the most difficult thing I have ever written because it deals with the events of September 11, 2001. It is a day that none of us shall ever forget. I was on the phone with a co-worker in the World Trade Center when he told me that he had to go because a plane just crashed into the building and they had to evacuate. Shortly after the phone lines went completely dead. I remember people seeking me out in the office to pray for loved ones that they believed were trapped inside. It was an odd surreal event to be under attack as a nation never knowing when the next plane was going to go down. Anger, rage, and indescribable pain and loss mingled together in that moment and throughout the days, weeks, and months that followed. War was declared shortly after and now ten years come this September 2011 our children are still fighting. It changed this nation forever, and is a somber reminder that our continued freedom is not free of charge.

PRICE OF FREEDOM

Across the ages the cry has gone out from the masses, "Give us Freedom!"
To those who have been willing to pay the price, it has been won.

Still, countless others continue to cry out for this most precious treasure.
Nowhere on earth does freedom shine so bright than in America.

The masses have come to this country from antiquity through today.
Covering every race, creed, and color all seeking one thing, Freedom!
We have struggled within our border to refine it for all peoples.
It has been bought and paid for with the lifeblood of countless known, and
unknown heroes, that have sacrificed not for glory or fame, but for the love of
freedom.

There are those who believed that Americans would no longer pay freedom's
price.
Yet, when attacked the world soon discovered that America would stand firm
holding sacred their Freedom.
For the cost has been too dear to let it slip away into the ashes of one fateful day.

In memoriam September 11, 2001

First published "The Best Poems and Poets of 2002" Int'l Library of Poetry ©
2002 ISBN# 0-7951-5175-6

A Team is a Symphony in Perpetual Motion was originally written for my company's newsletter. My company was struggling to merge to different cultures to make one cohesive business unit. I wrote this to encourage my fellow employees in that coming together didn't have to mean losing what made them special. The management at the time was so moved that they had it put on two plaques. One was presented to me, and the other was hung on the wall in the office to remind everyone of what a team was. It was a very moving ceremony and our Vice President actually broke into tears when he read the poem aloud to the staff.

A TEAM IS A SYMPHONY IN PERPETUAL MOTION

A team is a symphony in perpetual motion. It is made up of individuals just as an orchestra is made up of various instruments. Every instrument is unique, and although each one is beautiful on its own merit, its dimensions are limited to its specific characteristics.

In a symphony, instruments come together to produce something that none of them could produce alone. Likewise, individuals come together as a team to accomplish things that none could do on their own.

Teams at times seem to swallow the person. One for all, and all for one so to speak. This can, at times, be what destroys a team. When we forget the individuals that combine to form this thing we call a team, we are dangerously close to losing that which made the group special.

Symphonies have melodies, harmony, rhythm, and various styles. Not every instrument plays at the same time, nor is every note part of the melody. Yet you can't remove a single note or instrument from its moment or the desired effect will be crippled or even lost.

Individuals, like instruments, must take the time to tune themselves. A constantly changing world demands that we take the time to improve ourselves. We owe that to ourselves, and to those whose lives we touch on a daily basis. Technically a team is an intangible concept solely dependent upon our perception of what it should be, as well as our participation. Sometimes that participation is in the forefront, and at times it is quiet support in the background. Whatever its form, its importance can't and shouldn't be diminished.

Just like notes in a symphony, we as individual team members don't always play every measure. We must, however, keep constant count so as not to loose our place. For when our turn comes, our contribution will add the power and grace of a perfectly tuned orchestra playing a fantastic symphony.

FAITH

Angel's Keep is a feel good story about a guardian angel that takes care of a sick woman until she can be reunited with her family. I've always been encouraged by stories of people who have had encounters with angels. It's evidence that providence is working amongst us and that individual lives are part of a much greater tapestry then we realize. It is also a source of great encouragement in a world that is often times overwhelmingly dark and hopeless. This short story was donated to, "Writers for Relief II" published by Dragon Moon Press which supports the Bay Area Food Bank. This story is also the basis for our next short film project. I developed a fifteen minute screenplay based upon this story. This project is far less ambitious than Perfect copy was, but even so it has proven to have challenges of its own. Upon this writing principal photography has already begun with a multi-ethnic cast and assistance from Nicola Cuti's production company.

ANGEL'S KEEP

Karen Winslow was driving home from an out of town business meeting late on a Friday night. The roads were hazardous due to a torrential rainstorm that she drove right into about an hour ago, and there were no signs that the storm would be subsiding any time soon. In addition, she was achy and feverish suffering from the flu. The only lights besides the occasional lightning flash were those on her compact car. Just when things couldn't get any worse for Karen, the oil light on her car came on.

"Oh great, just what I need," Karen muttered. She knew she had been forgetting to do something, and now realized that she had been spacing taking her car in to be serviced. Her car was over ten years old, and when the idiot light comes on you better find a station. Unfortunately, nothing was open nor was she familiar with this stretch of deserted country back road. Dark takes on a whole new meaning in the mountains.

She thought she should telephone her husband to let him know that she may be delayed because she knew her car was about out of steam. She grabbed the cell phone and went to dial when she noticed that the battery had died. After fishing for the charger, she realized that she left it on the dining room table at home.

"Could this day get any worse? I didn't clinch the deal, I'm sick, my car's oil light just came on, and my cell phone is dead," Karen expounded amid coughs to the little dog attached to her dashboard. Suddenly the car's engine just stopped.

"Oh crap," she said aloud as the car slowed to a stop. The rain was coming down even harder now, and there was no one else on the road. She turned her flashers on in hopes that someone would come by, but no one did.

She sat there for about an hour, but didn't notice a light shining amongst the trees until after a spell of coughing had racked her entire body. The light caught her eye. She wiped the accumulated moister from the window with the sleeve of her blouse to get a clearer view of what the light was attached to. After staring intently for a moment, she realized that the light was attached to a house. Thinking that someone might be able to help her, she got out of the car. By the time she made it to the covered porch she was soaked to the core. There were no lights on inside the house, nor did she see a car, but she knocked anyway.

"Hello," she called, while knocking. "Is anyone home?" No one responded. She slid down the door to the floor. Too weak to move, she remained there. Every joint and muscle in her body was hurting, and she was shivering. She felt her forehead, the temperature of which you could fry an egg on, just before she fell unconscious.

When she finally regained consciousness, she found herself lying on a long fluffy sofa in front of a blazing fire. There was a glass on a nearby table filled with water. When she went to feel her forehead there was a towel lying upon it. She took it in her hands and realized that someone must have found her and been taking care of her through the night. She sat up to get a better view of her surroundings. As she did her eyes caught the image of a man with long dark hair that hung straight down around his face. He was handsome, and was dressed in a white collared shirt and black pants. In his hands, he carried a tray of hot tea and toast.

"You're awake," he commented. "You had a hard night."

"Who are you?" Karen asked.

"My name is Leslie. What's yours?"

"Karen Winslow. Thank you for taking care of me."

"It's not everyday a beautiful woman is dropped on ones doorstep. How are you feeling?" Leslie asked, setting the tray down on the coffee table.

"I feel weak, but I'm alive."

"That's a good start. Your fever broke sometime around 3:00 a.m. Try to drink some tea, and then if you're feeling up to it try the toast."

"Thanks," she said, taking the tea from his hands. She carefully took a sip. She waited a moment before taking another sip. Then she remembered that her husband must be worried sick. "Do you have a phone? I need to call my husband. He must be worried sick about me."

"Sorry, I don't have those sorts of things. I live too far out. I took a look at your car. You're out of oil."

"Yeah, I know."

"I might have some in the shed out back. Once you're strong enough, and out of danger from passing out, I think we can get you to a station where you can call your husband."

"You're very kind, Leslie."

All of a sudden there could be heard several male voices coming from outside. One of them sounded distinctly like that of her husband. She could discern that they were looking at her car.

"It looks like that the Calvary has arrived," Leslie commented. He helped Karen off the sofa and walked her to the door.

"Ted?" Karen called.

Ted, Karen's husband, heard her voice and responded immediately motioning the officers to follow him.

"Karen?" he called back, and then saw her in the doorway of the old house. Ted ran toward her relieved to find her safe. Upon reaching her location he took her into his arms, hugged her, and kissed her all over her head.

"Boy am I glad to see you," Karen whispered into his ear.

"Baby, not half as glad as I am to see you. I thought I'd lost you."

"Leslie took care of me. He said my fever broke this morning at about 3:00 a.m."

One of the officers overheard her name her benefactor and questioned her.

"Mrs. Winslow. Whom are you talking about?"

"Leslie, the man who owns this house. He took me in and put me by the fireplace, and even made me tea."

"No one has lived here in over a hundred years."

"But," Karen began to speak. When she turned back around to look for Leslie she discovered no one there. The fireplace that had been blazing just a moment ago was cold. The warmth of a charming home was suddenly shrouded in the dust of a century of idleness. "But, he was here, and there was a fire blazing in the fireplace. He had made me tea and toast," she coughed again.

"Sweetheart, you've had a high fever for several hours. You sound as if you have pneumonia. Let's get you to a doctor."

Ted walked Karen back to his car. Karen didn't have an explanation for what had happened to her. Maybe she did dream it all. Her fever was very high. Although when she turned back around before getting into her husband's car, she thought she spied Leslie peering through the window smiling at her. She smiled back and then got into the car.

Karen did have pneumonia, and the doctor told Ted that it was a miracle that she didn't die in the night. Karen kept insisting that her benefactor, Leslie, had kept watch over her until Ted arrived. Although the doctor dismissed Karen's claims, Ted couldn't help but wonder if she had been in an Angel's keep.

Faith is a reflection of my own personal pursuit of God. It is the way I try to live my life. I have had many challenges throughout my life that has strengthened my belief in God through Jesus Christ. I do not hide this aspect of my life, nor apologize for it. I am what I am and people take me or leave me on that basis.

FAITH

Faith cannot be seen with the natural eye,
for its residence is the heart.

Faith cannot be felt in our emotions,
for it is not from ourselves.

Faith cannot be touched by the human hand,
for it is faith that touches us.

Faith is not bound by the laws of this existence,
for it harbors more power than anything in the universe.

Faith is a portion of Heaven given by God to His children.
It is impossible for your faith to be stolen.
It cannot be lost.
It can only be given away.

Faith is an unwavering trust in God,
That He will do what He says He will do.
That His Word is always and for all.

Most believe that Faith is needed only for miracles,
but in reality Faith is needed for every moment of our lives.

He's Already There was written for a contest for song lyrics. This song is my heart's testimony of what God is to me and who and what he has been in my life. I won the right to be published in an Anthology and was one of my earliest published works.

HE'S ALREADY THERE

In your darkest hour when death beckons more than life,
A Savior stands ready to lead you to the light.
He came to free the captive, heal the sick and save the lost.
Love was sent to pay the total cost.

Chorus
God's already there.
There's no need for Him to follow you, because God's already there.

Although you have fought the fight the battle rages on,
God stands ready to finish it simply give it to Him all.
He is with you always from now until the end.
He is the mighty hand that rescued you from Hell.

When life has left you thirsting for more than it can give,
Drink from the fount of living water that only He can give.
There are no complicated riddles, nor roads to be driven,
God is able to meet the needs of all His children.

First published in "On the Road Anthology" © 1998 The Association of
Songwriters & Lyricists
A Div. Of United Recording Artists Network

The Cradle and the Cross was written as a Christmas Poem to send to friends and family. It was one of the more popular things I've ever given at Christmas. This was also later published in "The Best Poems and Poets of 2001."

The Cradle and the Cross

The cradle was hewn with love and joy.
The cross was hewn with anger and hate.
The cradle was planed and sanded with care.
The cross was rough and cruel an instrument of death and pain.
The cradle holds the comfort of a mother's love.
The cross holds the defilement of sin.
Christ came by way of them both, to redeem the lives of men.
His cradle prepared Him to be one of us.
His cross, prepared us to be heirs with Him.
He paid the price that we could not.
What then can we give back in return?
To love God with all of our heart, soul, mind, and strength,
And to love one another just as He loves us.
He counted the cross the way we count the cradle,
But for the joy set before Him, he endured it all.

First published in "The Best Poems and Poets of 2001" ISBN:0-7951-5174-8

Today, Tomorrow, and Always was originally written to encourage a friend going through some difficulties. It lifted her spirits, and I hope that it will lift yours. It's a reminder that we are never alone and that God is mindful of our sorrows and desires to comfort us.

TODAY, TOMORROW, AND ALWAYS

Never let your doubt diminish your praise,
For in your praise I will heal.
Never let your troubles hush your worship,
For in your worship I will set free.
Never let your voice cease from calling my name,
For in your prayer I will listen and speak.

Those that have never seen the dark would not recognize the dawn.
O, child of my creation, I have rescued you from the dark.
I have set your feet on the path of righteousness for my name's sake.
I have sent my angels before you to keep your way clear.
Know that in the deepest reaches of your soul I abide with you.

My arm is not short that I can't deliver you into my joy.
Though the world crumbles around you, I will be your rock.
Though you may grow tired, I will be your strength.
Keep my Word in your heart and you will hear my voice.
Obey my voice and you will be blessed.

One was a revelation of singular acts enacted by God throughout time that have had eternal ramifications for mankind. It is simple yet profound to ponder these singular moments. Many times we tend to think of God as the big picture, but He is also in the details. When you really examine it you soon discover that the details add to the panorama of life so vividly and resolutely that they are the same.

ONE

The Lord our God is one.
With one word all of creation came into existence.
With one breath, you gave life to man.
With one decision man fell into sin.
With one voice you called us to repentance.
With one love you cared and provided for your people.
With one flood you judged the earth and started anew.
With one gift you declared your resolve to restore us.
With one sacrifice you provided atonement for all.
With one resurrection you conquered hell and the grave.
In one moment you will call us home.
The Lord our God is one, and for eternity we will be.